ILLUMINATING INVISIBLE
DISABILITIES THROUGH
TATTOO CULTURE

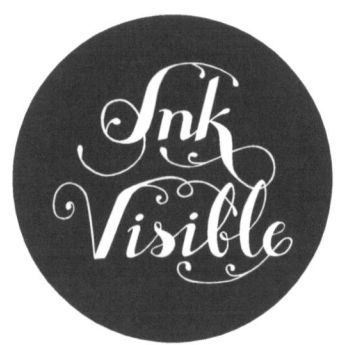

INKVISIBLE.ORG

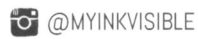 @MYINKVISIBLE

ABOUT

Ink Visible is a collection of temporary tattoos, an event series and a support network about invisible disabilities. Arianna Warner collaborates with tattoos artists in multiple cities to create temporary tattoos inspired by their lived experience with an invisible disability. Each tattoo artist's personal story accompanies their temporary tattoo which is distributed at each city's Ink Visible Public Event.

Invisible disabilities are disabilities that are not visually recognizable and manifest within each individual in different ways rather than in an easy identifiable pattern. Ink Visible is about sharing individual experiences and emphasises that while disabilities may be similar in nature, it does not mean that people feel and live with them in the same way.

There are stereotypes of what a person with a disability "should" look like, and when people with invisible disabilities do not fit that stigmatized perception, their invisible disability most often becomes irrelevant.

Ink Visible steps away from a "one size fits all" visual label and allows individuals to self-identify and generate awareness and understanding of invisible disabilities. While education plays a key role in catalysing a change within disability rights, it is very important to create space for individuals to contribute personal experience to this dialogue.

At each Ink Visible Public Event Arianna invites the public to add their story to the collection by contributing their own page to the book. Each book acts as a record and an educational resource from each city that represents some of the lived experiences of its resident tattoo artists and locals. In doing so, Ink Visible illuminates invisible disabilities through tattoo culture.

Portland, Oregon is the first Ink Visible city featuring Lindsay Carter (Opal Ink), Aubrey Hight (Hawthorne Ink), Tanya Magdalena (Above the Pearl Tattoo LLC), Kimber Teatro (Hawthorne Ink), and Trevor Ward (Albatross Tattoo).

Additional Ink Visible collaborators include Paige Buda, Ink Visible Graphic Designer, and Nadine Edwards, Ink Visible Intern.

Throughout this booklet are the stories and drawings contributed to Ink Visible. The first page is by Kimber Teatro, Ink Visible Tattoo Artist. The following pages were collected at the Portland Ink Visible Public Event from participants. By creating books full of participants individual stories we are able to share and learn about different experiences.

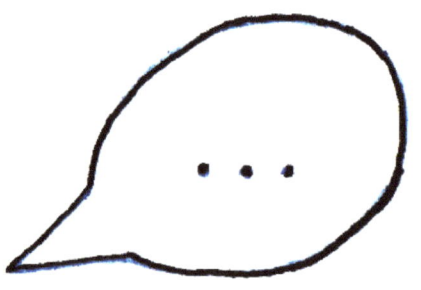

Anke Schüttler

Aachen, Germany
Language Barriers

When you first meet me you might be impressed by the fact that I speak your language almost fluently, no I wanted to say perfectly (?)... but then you might soon see me struggle find words, depending on the time of day, situation or level of fatigue. Ever since coming to America I have encountered many frustrating moments where I could not say as precisely as I wished what I wanted to say because of language barriers, lack of vocabulary, not finding the exact right word in the exact right moment... also my own language, German becomes less precise by being far away from it so long. I almost imagine this situation as having almost an equal amount of words you can carry in your brain at all times.

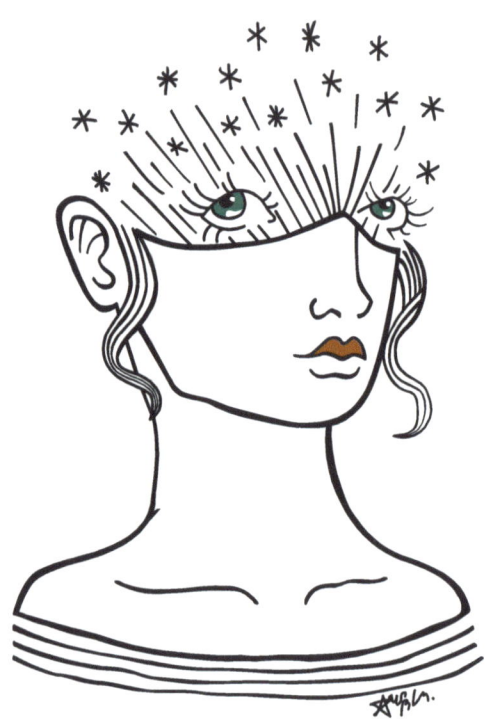

Aubrey Hight

Portland, OR

Depression

This image is a visual interpretation of my "invisible illness"
which is depression. A lot of people have this convoluted idea
of what depression "looks" like. They see the media make
it seem like a person who just cries all day. In reality, it is
different for many people. For me I feel out of my body, I feel
lonely and hopeless. A lot of my life has been affected by my
depression, it's a constant battle. It is more than an "intense
sadness". Hence the image of a person whose mind is vast,
like space. Often space is described as lonely as well. I hope
this image and description is helpful to someone also suffer-
ing from depression.

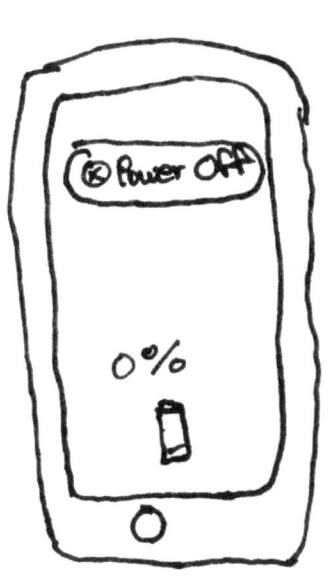

Carly

Portland, OR

Chronic Migraines, A.D.H.D.,
Depression, Anxiety

I've had migraines since I was 14 years old. Many times
it would interfere with my school work and attendance,
and I was constantly told to suck it up or stop pretending
or stop begging for attention. When I turned 16 I became
very depressed, and I have been trying to fend off the dark
demons of melancholy and apathy ever since. It's difficult to
convince myself to spend time with people that I really enjoy,
and more difficult to do things like work and school. When I
get migranes now, they are always followed by panic attacks
and low points about what I've had to miss because of them.
I often try to ignore all the outside factors in my life, which
usually just perpetuates my depression further.

Cheryl

Portland, OR

Traumatic Brain Injury

The most important part of my story, I think, is that it's mine. I'm constantly amazed by the entitlement people feel to the personal stories of disabled people. When people ask for "my story", they typically mean, "Tell me about your wreck. Car wreck? Bike wreck? Coma?" Years later, people ask what deficits I still have that I'm working on in rehab. Actually, I'm working on learning filmmaking techniques, undoing toxic family communication patterns, and how to find joy in things like this Ink Visible event that would have overloaded my vision and hearing to the point of collapse just a few years ago. I'm learning joy, compassion, social justice, and mindfulness. I'm learning to say- when strangers demand a graphic crash story to say, with no emotion, "I don't need to tell that story. I don't need to talk about that. I want to talk about art or cats or Closed Captions." My story is disability community and pride and my utterly beautiful, nourishing love of activists, disabled folks working for equity, and actually, cats.

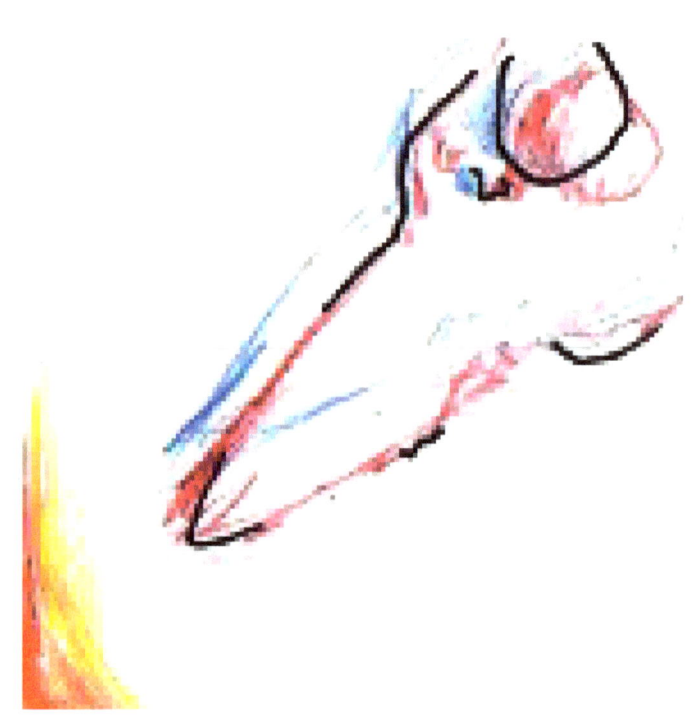

Claire Aldridge

Portland, OR

Anxiety, Depression, ADHD & they aren't quite sure yet.

I started hallucinating when I was 14. I would be lying if I said I wasn't terrified. They got in the way of everything. I didn't get diagnosed with depression until I was 17. Then they said anxiety, also ADHD, but the hallucinations? The arrows, the shadows, the colors. Shit, they have no idea.

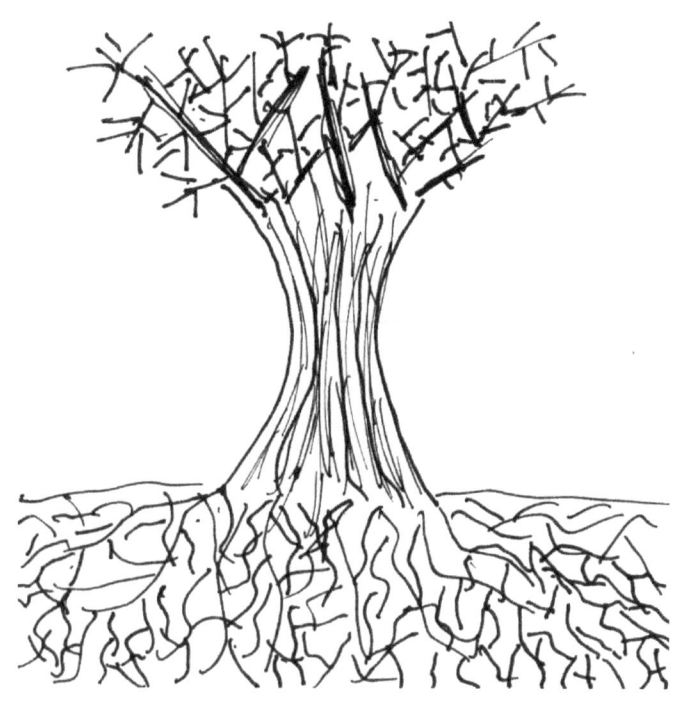

Elizabeth Findley

Arcata, CA

P.O.T.S., Chronic Pain, Depression & Anxiety

It was hard for me to even begin thinking that there was something wrong. I developed my symptoms at the age of 14 after officially being depressed for a year. I looked fine. I looked healthy. But there was so much going on under the hood. Everyone assumed I was being lazy or trying to get attention. If it wasn't for my sister (unfortunately with the same condition as me) and my mother for pushing for more answers, I wouldn't be here today.

I'm managing my life now as a college student. And everyday I'm reminded of the things I missed being sick. But now I'm at a great point in my life. Because three years earlier, a girl dried off tears, took a chance, and hoped.

I make the same decision every day. Whether or not to stay in bed and just accept who I've become. But I've made it this far and learned that things can actually be worth it.

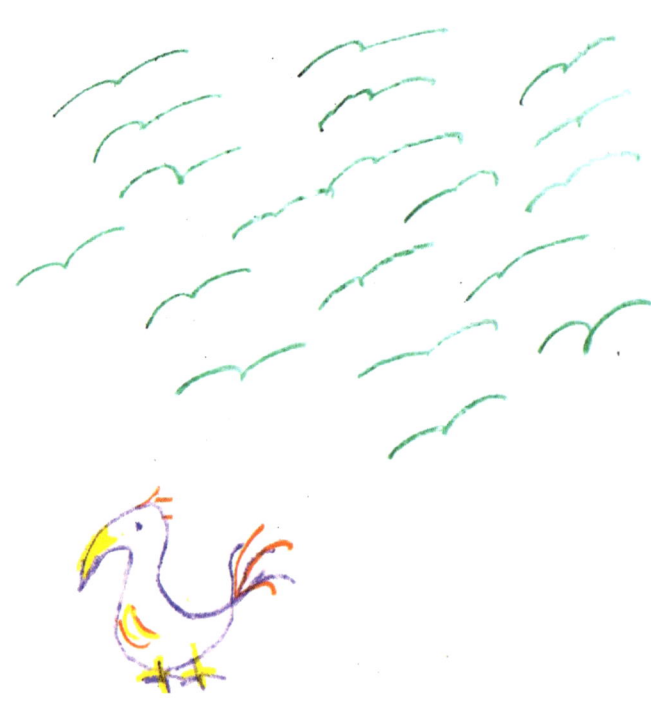

Jennie

Portland, OR

Borderline Personality Disorder

I love you
I hate you
Please don't leave me
Go away
You are wrong
I am right
I am wrong
You are right
There is no grey
I have no fight

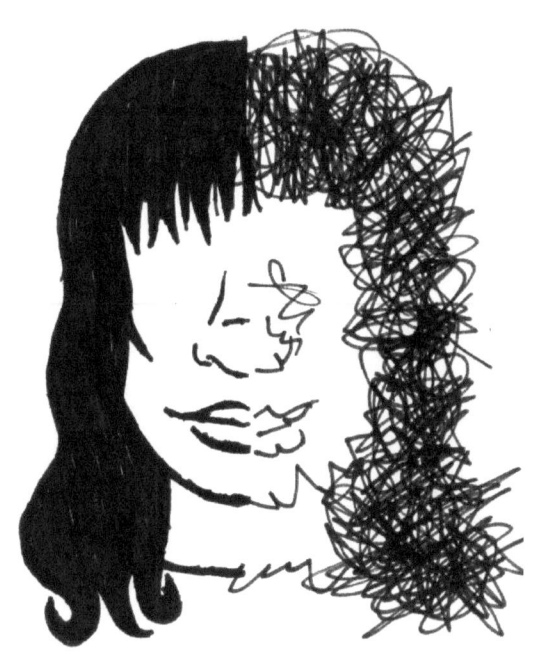

Jordan Shelton

Portland, OR

Borderline Personality Disorder

As an adolescent, depression and anxiety was always something I struggled with. It wasn't until I was 20 that I was diagnosed with Borderline Personality Disorder. I realized that my depression and anxiety were just a fraction of a bigger problem. Any sort of "disorder" is overwhelming, but I've learned that it really does make me who I am. It makes me sensitive, creative, full of love, and self aware. It's more of a "characteristic" than it is a "disorder." I have tried to look at it positively. Sometimes, it really is terrible, but I've learned to utilize it to the best of my ability. My Disorder is my superpower.

Jose Ruiz

Portland, OR

T-4 Paraplegic

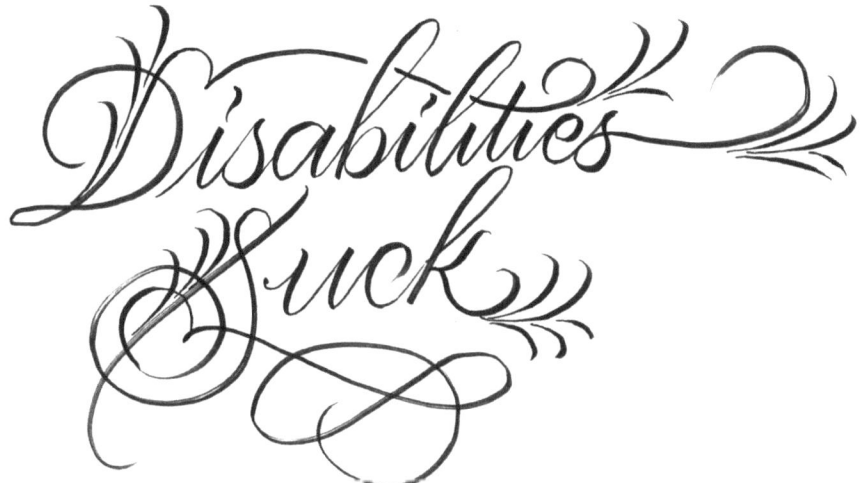

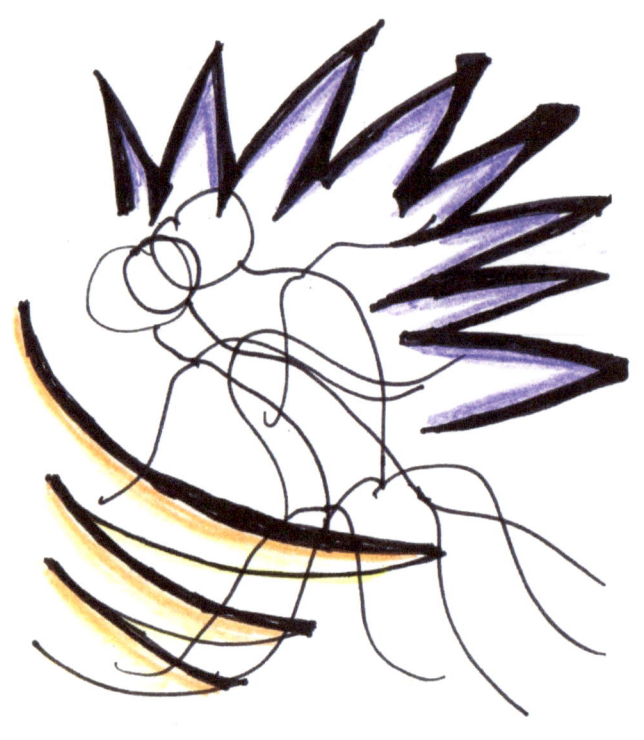

Kate

Portland, OR

E.D.N.O.S.

I was diagnosed with E.D.N.O.S. (Eating Disorder Not Otherwise Specified) in April of 2006. I was fortunate to have parents that could afford to spend time on my treatment. I was extremely closed off about it, and the disorder put distance between me and everyone I loved- most notably, my best friends and sister. I still feel angry for the years and love it took from me while I felt completely isolated and alone. Knowledge really was my power. As I got older, I learned more about what had happened to me and why. I now know that millions of other people suffered in the same way. It is the best and worst thing that has ever happened to me.

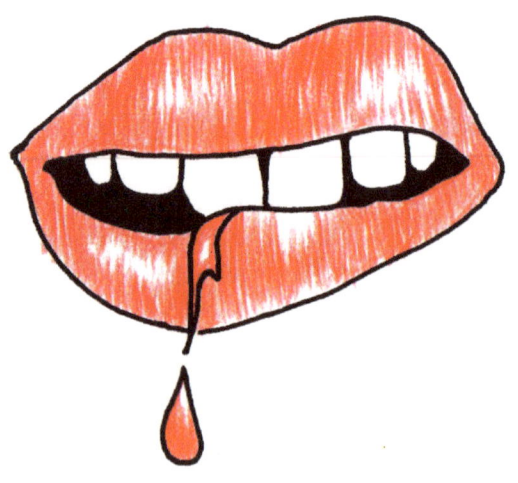

Kaylee Van Emmerik
Portland, OR
O.C.D. Cheek Biting

Although Cheek Biting is the common term, it's not exclusive to just cheeks. Without knowing it, I'll be biting my lips, cheeks and tongue. Telling myself to stop never works and even chewing gum doesn't alleviate it. I don't even know what my trigger for it is. I could be reading a book, with friends or listening to music and once I start, it's very difficult to stop. Every part of my mouth hurts after that. Eating, talking, drinking and even brushing my teeth becomes painful. It's gotten to the point to where I don't even feel it half the time. And it's gotten so bad that I've bit to the fatty layer of my cheek. Nobody sees this. I don't talk about it. I've always just dealt with it. Only twice in my life have I been able to stop and keep my mouth unharmed for more than two weeks. I hope to find a "cure" for this one day. For now I'll keep trying gum.

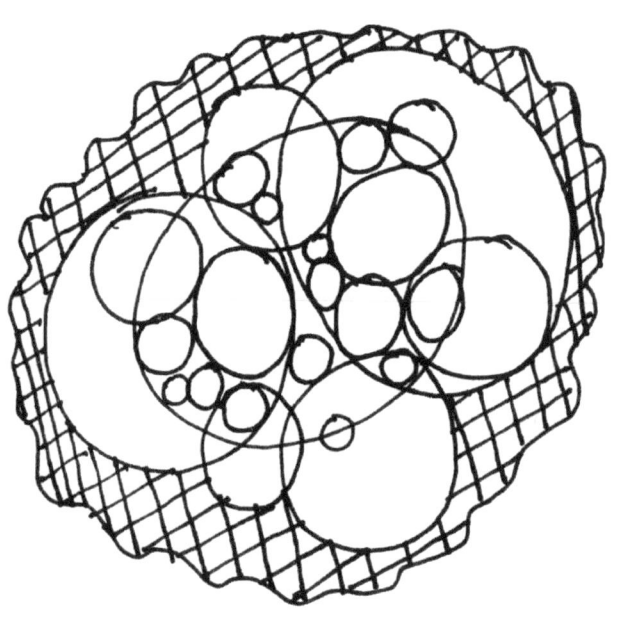

Kevin

Calgary, AB
Repressed Collectivist

I...
I...
I...
We begin our stories with "I". It's the most used pronoun in our english language.
We are told that we can be whoever we want to be right from our first class of Kindergarten.
We are told that we must try hard - climb that ladder; overcome that obstacle; be strong!

I want to live amongst the we.
I want to recognize that their is power in the we.
I want to believe that there is something beyond the we.

It's NOT SOCIALISM!
It's about caring for the stranger I just met walking down Quimby NW in Portland.
It's about having empathy for others.

I want to tell you - I love the we!
We want to tell you - we love you!

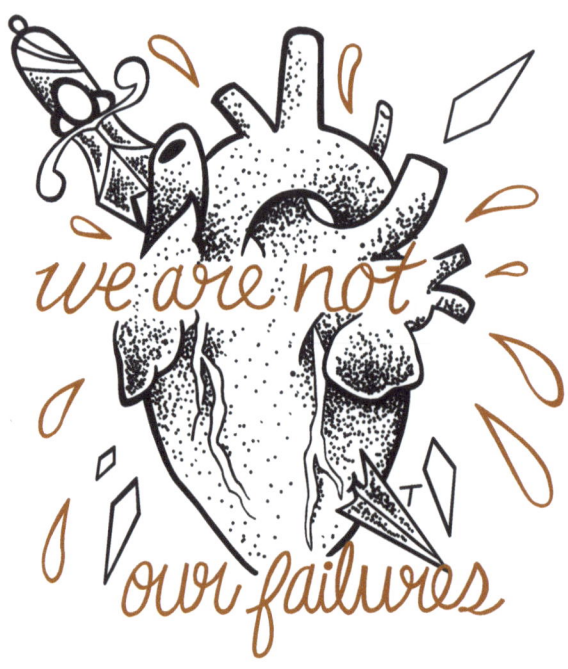

Kimber Teatro
Portland, OR
Depression

"Self Harm"

I'll never be able to explain why at the bottom of everything. To make myself hurt is the only way to make myself feel better. Growing up I was constantly told my depression was just a "phase" that I need to just "get over it..." How do you get over something you don't fully understand? Something you can't see but know it's there? Something everyone demeans about you until you shut the fuck up about it and stop asking for help.

I am not perfect.

But I am a constant work in progress.

I am turning my self loathing into energy showing people I can do what they always said I wouldn't. It's an everyday battle but, through tattooing I'm learning to love myself.

Your feelings have validation.

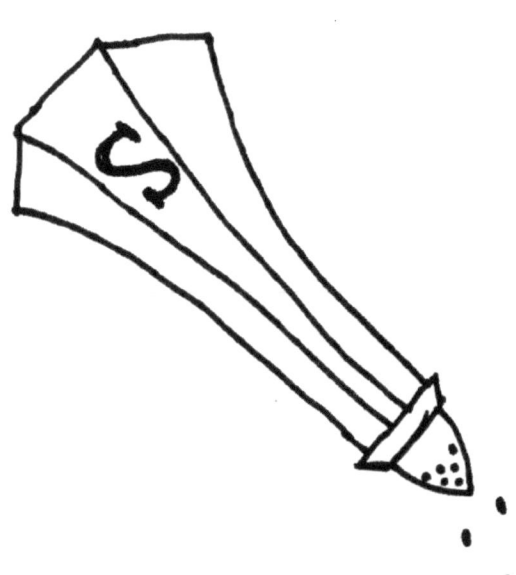

Lacy Findley

Portland, OR

P.O.T.S., Chronic Pain,
Migraines, Depression

Throughout my life, I knew something was wrong. I couldn't explain what was going on, I just knew my body wasn't working the way it should. When I was 17, I had my first encounter with chronic pain. Doctor after doctor tried to help, eventually getting too frustrated with the girl who didn't get better. Diagnosis after diagnosis came and went. I dropped out of high school and withdrew into my shell. But in that dark time, a support group for chronically ill teenagers found me. Through the support of others like me, living with invisible pain, I felt like I could master my pain. The pain hasn't left me, and I doubt it ever will. But that pain is a part of me now, and it resonates within me everyday.

My autonomic nervous system disorder demands that I eat a lot of salt. I happily comply.

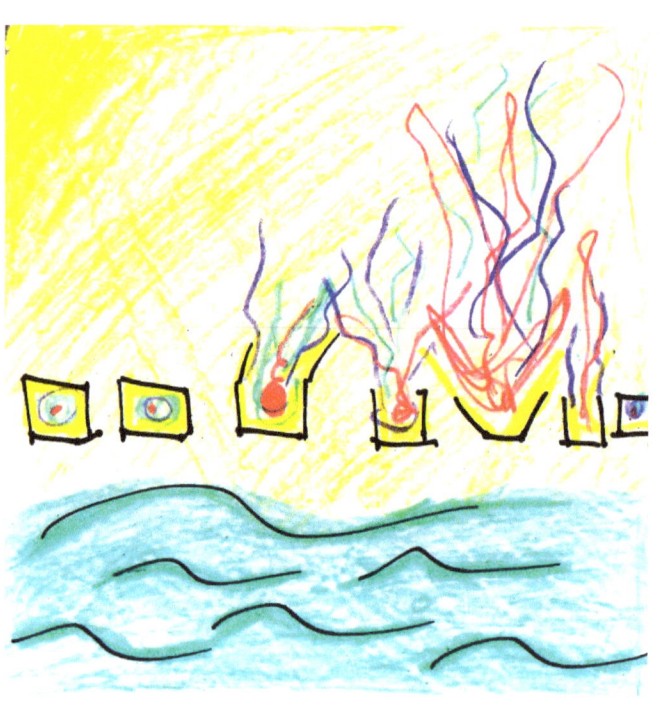

Lauren Crombie

Portland, OR

Anxiety

Structure feels safe to me. I have often dealt with anxiety as young as eleven years old. I can really remember dealing with it. I have a difficult time dealing with change and unexpected events. At that age I quickly felt like a difficult child because my parents didn't know how to handle my anxiety and sent me to a therapist. I still deal with it but I have built some skills around handling worrisome thoughts, it takes work, but is helpful.

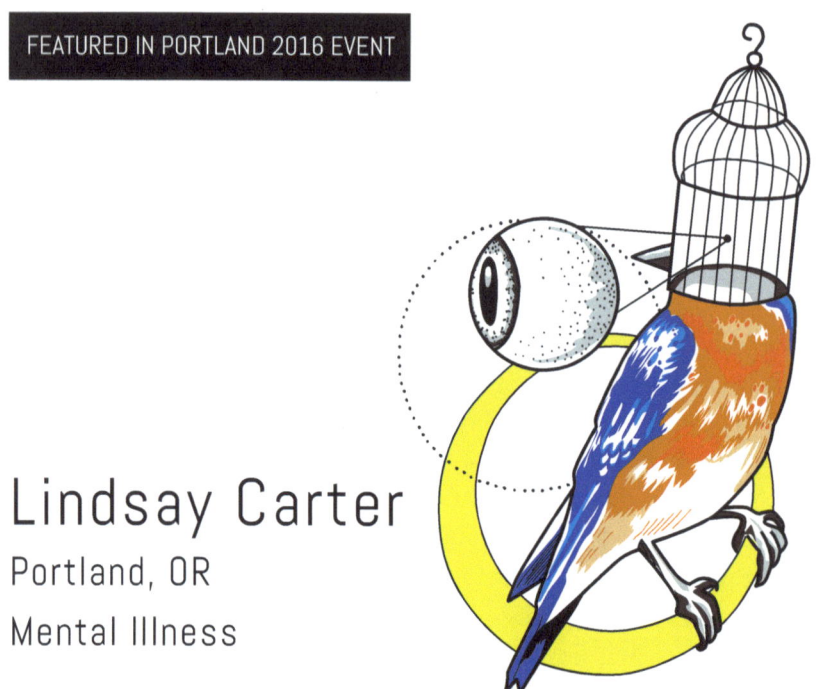

Lindsay Carter
Portland, OR
Mental Illness

I have chosen a surreal art approach to represent my invisible disability, due to the surreal nature of mental illness. As long as I've been consciously aware, I've been diagnosed with generalized anxiety disorder and major depressive disorder. On the Carter side of my inheritance, mental disorders are of no surprise. The difference between me and someone without a supposed genetic influence is that mine seems to be a life-long process, and not always situational. Severe episodes can happen for no apparent reason and at that point I cannot help nor snap out of the exaggerated feelings. I subjectively illustrate mental illness as being caged within your own mind.

I have plenty of recollections in my childhood home of being comforted by bird chirps in my Mom's garden, which is where the choice of a bird in this piece has become personable. My most severe episodes of anxiety, panic attacks, and depression occurred back home and birds were sometimes the only outdoor life I'd see beyond the couch I'd spend excessive amounts of time isolating and sleeping on (a common symptom of depression). The choice of the blue bird itself was a common sight in the garden, and in this particular design it inherently represents how I've acquired a "bad case of the blues"; something completely out of my control.

At a vulnerable age of 14 my anxiety and depression took a twist and I developed depersonalization and derealization disorder. The first experience with this at age 14 was painfully severe and was a lasting and sedating disturbance for many months; it took some adjusting to my new reality to feel comfortable. They say those who develop this have a supposed genetic predisposition, and can be triggered later in life. It is a very subjective disorder, and hard to describe to those whom have not experienced it. It's marked by periods of feeling disconnected or detached from one's body and actions, as if you are observing yourself from outside your body or like being in a dream. It can fog your memory and make one numb to everything and everyone around them. However, you do not lose contact with reality and know things are not as they appear.

My derealization/depersonalization makes me feel alien to this world. The eye ball separate or "disconnected" from the bird is relevant to my experience with this disorder. Sometimes all I feel attached to is an eyeball of which observes everything else that's existing in the "real" reality. Sometimes my hands and arms and don't look like they are mine. I've described it as feeling enclosed in a bubble, and the reality everyone else is still connected to is on the other side. The circles in the design abstractly suggest a bubble of which warps perception and makes my vision foreign. Since the trigger at age 14, this disorder is still ongoing. Whilst plenty of symptoms still play into my day to day life, when anxiety levels are down I do not find it as emotionally disruptive as it was at 14. Not feeling connected has oddly enough become my own normality after years of experiencing it, and it's said that one can live with it for a matter of days or years.

There were many occasions I was not okay with these disorders and I let all of this define me and engulf me. I had wished brain transplants were common, so I could drive a luxurious "normal" one right off the lot. Over the years of feeling somewhat defective, I've grown to accept and appreciate my disorders for assisting me in who I am today. There's a great relief in knowing you're not alone. There really is a population whom have invisible complexities and these people are still thriving. For me, all of my complexities have given me such a great insight on life valuing and stretch my artistic mind. This cage fits snug, and I'm not sure what I'd be without it.

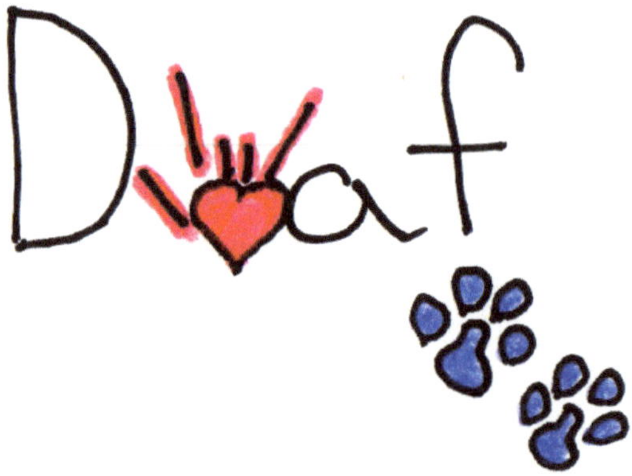
Deaf

Michele Howard

Vancouver, WA
Deaf

I grew up as Deaf and I have to face with a lot of people who make assumptions such as think I can hear by raise voices or think I am blind where they hand me the braille menu at restaurant. People always try to talk to me thinking I am hearing until I tell them I am Deaf. Sometimes people tried to talk to me and I didn't hear them and they would think I am rude. Now, I finally have a dog to support me and to be my ears.

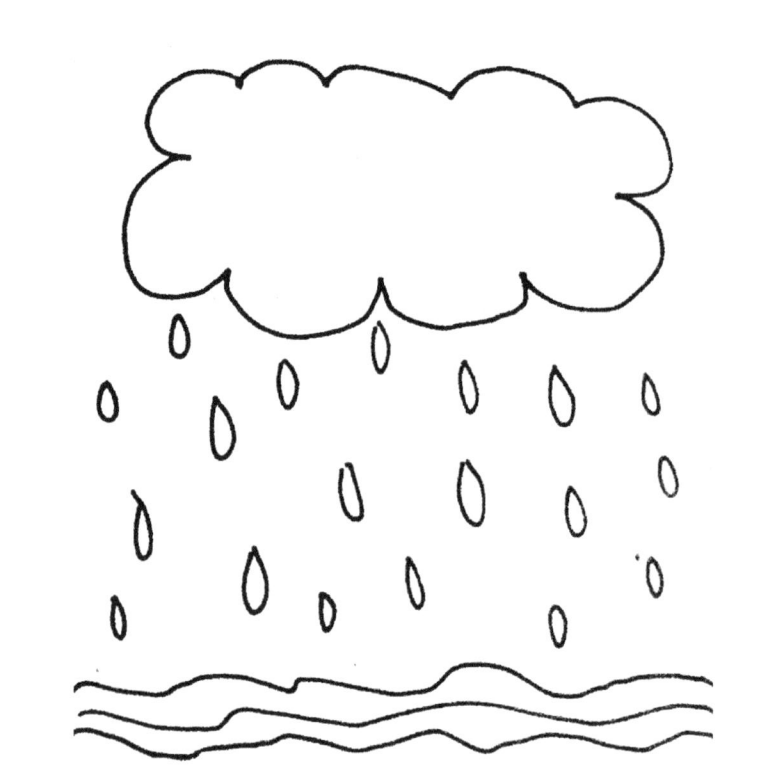

Nadine

Portland, OR

Major Depressive Disorder

Deep, deep sadness is where I'm most comfortable. In this
alternate reality I am scared and alone.

 I am drowning.

  14 years.

  7 days in.

This still hasn't escaped me.

You'll be with me forever.

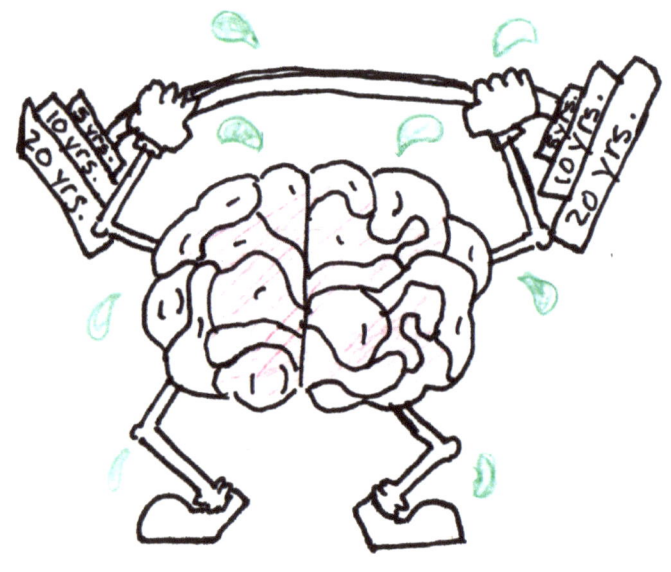

Omar R.
Portland, OR
A.D.H.D.

I've always been ambitious. In my academics, activities, work. I didn't realize until my sophomore year of college that there was an issue. My work load would stay the same, but it got harder and harder to do. I was later diagnosed with A.D.H.D. At that moment, it all made sense. Now, I channel my disability in my creative outlet- video.

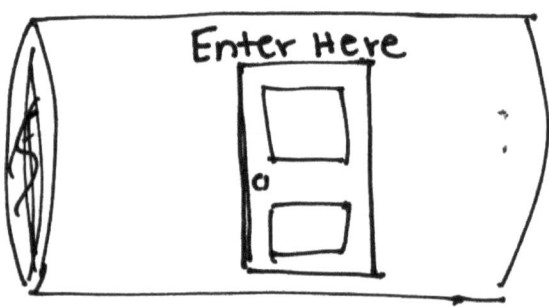

Rachel
Portland, OR
Chronic Tonsillitis and Sleep Apnea

I have struggled with year-round allergies all my life.
Doctors have prescribed countless meds and still I struggle.
In my junior year of college, I began having tonsillitis.
Today, three years later, my tonsillitis is chronic. They
alternate between being so swollen that it brings me to
tears just to swallow saliva, and being sollen that they
nearly touch. I struggled with explaining to people how
much it affected me until I did a sleep study and got con-
crete proof. I have moderate to, at times, severe sleep
apnea. This means I literally stop breathing several times
throughout the night. Sleep used to be one of my favorite
things to do, and now, I could sleep more than 24 hours and
still wake up exhausted. Sleep used to be my sanctuary from
all my stress and worries. Now, with a diagnosis. Someday
soon it will be my sanctuary again.

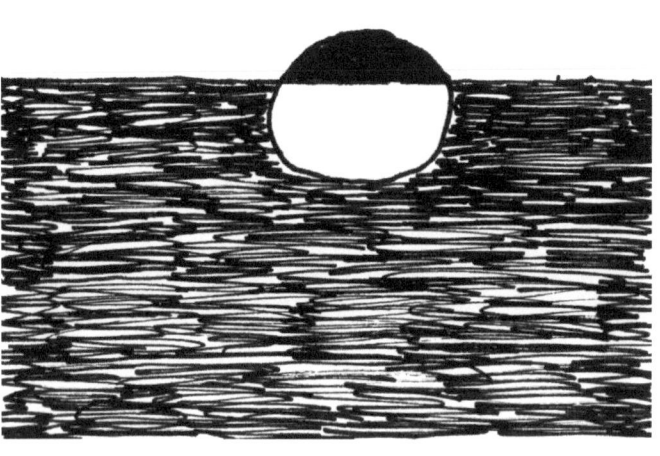

Randel Moore

Salem, OR

A.D.D., Anxiety, Depression

I have always had a very difficult time concentrating on scholastic activities. No matter how hard I tried, no matter how much I wanted to, I was never able to just sit down and do my homework. The more I struggled the more anxious I would become. The more I failed to meet my potential, the more depressed I became. Doctors did their best to help, but the medicines only gave me side effects. The counselors did their best, but they couldn't make me better. In the end I decided that traditional education wasn't make for me, or me for it. Although I eventually graduated I look back on what were supposed to be my best years, as my most bitter.

I still struggle with A.D.D. and anxiety but I have learned to play to my strengths and rely on others to help in the areas I am lacking. Maybe this way I can find a way to be successful. Today I still need help to do what others find easy. Maybe I always will.

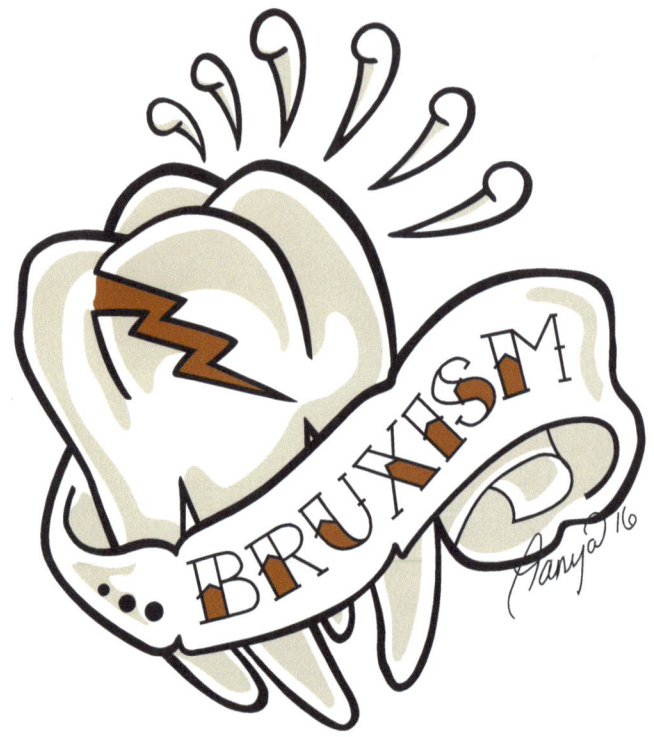

Tanya Magdelena

Portland, OR

Bruxism & T.M.J.

Bruxism (BRUK-siz-um) is a condition in which you grind, gnash or clench your teeth. Bruxism makes you unconsciously clench your teeth together during the day (awake bruxism), or clench or grind them at night (sleep bruxism). In some people, bruxism can be frequent and severe enough to lead to jaw disorders (TMJ), headaches, damaged teeth and other problems. There is currently no 'cure' for bruxism.

While I have a perfectly healthy mouth, gums and pristine oral hygiene, I kill my teeth by unconsciously beating them to death. Even with a night guard, and sometimes wearing it during the day, I am plagued with root canals and broken teeth. Stress and bruxism go hand in hand.

Tattooing is stressful. I love what I do. I am in my 11th year of full time tattooing, am a one-woman show, and own my own business/studio. I was a graphic designer for 15 years prior to tattooing. After burning out in a corporate blaze of glory, I pursued my childhood dream of becoming a tattooer.

Tattooing is a moral and ethical responsibility. I, and all tattooers, are exposed everyday to the public, their fears, excitements, psychosis, indecisions, certainty, bodies, and body fluids. We put our health, and safety, on the line daily, to adorn your beautiful selves.

I cause you pain and make you bleed. I bring your body and spirit to its limit. I make your whole body flood with natural chemicals, that make you question, panic, resign, endure, and elate, in a cathartic release. I permanently install images under your skin that will be there for as long as you exist, sometimes longer, depending on your chosen method of disposal. I am inside your body, penetrating your skin. I change you. I counsel you. I cleanse you. I am your stranger confidant. I keep your secrets. I facilitate your rite-of-passage. I am with you for the rest of your life. It is a hefty responsibility. I know this, and love, and hugely respect every minute of it. I take what I do very seriously, making sure my clients get exactly what they want, so a great deal of stress in inherent.

While the physical act of tattooing itself, is very Zen, the process leading up to the moment of installation can be an arduous journey. A lot of the job is trying to save people from themselves, one tattoo at a time. What helps keep the stress down is having clients who are prepared, punctual, listen to advice, think long-term, keep their appointments, tip, and are kind and respectful of my time, knowledge and efforts.

So, be nice and respectful to your tattoo artist, whomever it may be. It will come back to you three-fold, and possibly save a tooth! Happy tattoos!

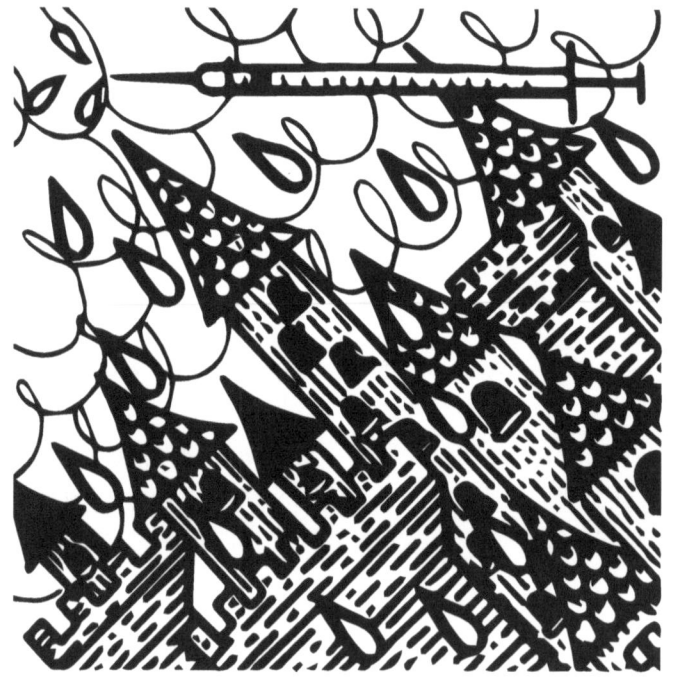

Trevor Ward

Portland, OR

Diabetes

I was diagnosed with diabetes when I was 8 years old. I remember my brother Dan and I were sick at the same time, he got better and I didn't. I went to the doctor the next day and Dr. Chochinov told me "You're going to do your own shot today". This was quite exciting and unexpected for my 8 year old self. I think that was the best thing he could have done for me. It was such a blessing that I could do my own injections and go for sleepovers and be a kid. In elementary school, I remember going into the office at lunchtime to check my blood sugars, which was more of a process than it is now days. The tools and insulins we have now are so much better than it was back then. Being diabetic has never stopped me from doing anything I wanted to do, I wake every morning and start my day just as everyone does, I just have a few more things to take care of than others. I am blessed to live and have been diagnosed in an age where diabetes would have previosuly been a death sentence. Now the only thing dyingis my bank account, as it is crazy expensive for the fancy medication, even with insurance. The image I drew up was what looked to me to be something fun to tattoo. I didn't draw it with too much thought about meaning but I suppose if I thought about it I would be the castle and the rain or storm "diabetes" would come down but with the right attitude it won't do too much damage to me, the castle.

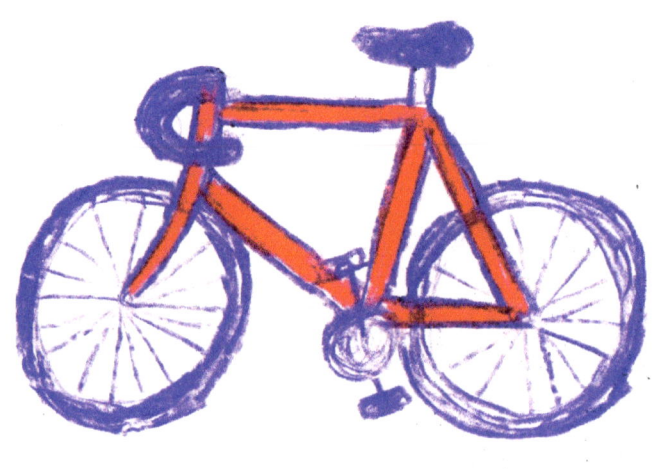

Zachary

Milwaukie, OR

Scoliosis

I often have back pain but I don't let it get the best of me.
I bike and am very active and am grateful for these joys.
Biking represents freedom from being disabled.

KICKSTARTER FUNDED

Ultimate Kickstarter Supporters:
Veronica Ramaci
Robyn Robinson
Bob and Kim Warner

RESOURCES

Ink Visible
Inkvisible.org
@myinkvisible

Arianna Warner
Ariannawarner.com

Paige Buda
Paigebuda.com
@paigebuda

Lindsay Carter
Tattoosbylindsaycarter.com
@lindsayraecarter

Aubrey Hight
Tattoosbyaubrey.tumblr.com
@spoopyspaghetti

Tanya Magdalena
abovethepearl.com

Kimber Teatro
@kimberteatro
@pdxcrybabies

Trevor Ward
Albatrosstattoo.com
@trevorward